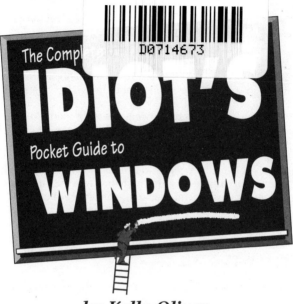

The Complete **IDIOT'S** Pocket Guide to **WINDOWS**

by Kelly Oliver

alpha books

A Division of Prentice Hall Computer Publishing
11711 North College Avenue, Carmel, Indiana 46032 USA

For my sisters, Sharyn, Debbie, and Laura. May the sun above you always shine as brightly as you do.

International Standard Book Number:1-56761-302-0
Library of Congress Catalog Card Number: 93-71927

95   9   8   7   6

Interpretation of the printing code: the rightmost number of the first series of numbers is the year of the book's printing; the rightmost number of the second series of numbers is the number of the book's printing. For example, a printing code of 93-1 shows that the first printing of the book occurred in 1993.

Screen reproductions in this book were created by means of the program Collage Plus from Inner Media, Inc., Hollis, NH.

Printed in the United States of America

Publisher, Marie Butler-Knight; **Associate Publisher**, Lisa A. Bucki; **Managing Editor**, Elizabeth Keaffaber; **Acquisitions Manager**, Stephen R. Poland; **Development Editor**, Sherry Kinkoph; **Manuscript Editor**, San Dee Phillips; **Cover Designer**, Jean Bisesi; **Designer**, Kevin Spears; **Indexer**, Jeanne Clark; **Production Team**, Diana Bigham, Katy Bodenmiller, Brad Chinn, Scott Cook, Tim Cox, Meshell Dinn, Mark Enochs, Howard Jones, Tom Loveman, Beth Rago, Carrie Roth, Greg Simsic

Contents

Introduction

Looking Through Your Windows

When I Was Your Age, a Candy Bar Was a Nickel

People seem to be fascinated with the advances of technology. If your elders are anything like mine, they are constantly telling stories about the first time they saw a television set or their family's first private phone line. Some day, that person telling stories of the good old days will be you. You'll have the rapt attention of all the children who can't imagine life without VCRs and video games, and you'll look down into their little awe-filled faces and say, "I remember when Windows came out."

Come On, Is Windows Really Such a Major Event?

Plain and simply, Windows is a *big deal*. The hugest of deals. It has changed the PC world forever. If you've had to work with DOS or another operating system for an extended period of time, I think you will agree. Oh sure, you can do a lot of handy things with DOS and you don't actually *need* Windows to get by. But why use DOS when Windows is so much better? It's like comparing a twelve year-old black and white televsion that only gets one channel with a brand-new big-screen color T.V. It's bigger and prettier, and all your neighbors will envy you if you have it.

Windows is incredibly easy to use once you get the hang of it. You don't have to type in any commands (like you do at the DOS command prompt) because you choose them from menus. You can even use your mouse to select commands. With this book as a guide, you'll soon be a whiz at using Windows. You'll learn about icons, groups, windows, documents, print queues, file management, and applications. If you want to learn quickly and don't have time to bother with the details (and, frankly, don't care about the details), then the *Complete Idiot's Pocket Guide to Windows* is for you.

How to Use This Book

The *Complete Idiot's Pocket Guide to Windows* is designed to be a friendly, easy-to-use manual for those of us who need to know the basics about using Windows, or just want something to put in our pockets. Each lesson is short and to the point and is written with a conversational tone so you won't feel like you have to read each sentence twelve times to understand it.

There are special little features like tips and figures that will help you along the way. You can look at the figures to see examples of the way your screen should look when you perform certain commands or follow a set of instructions.

The tips look like this:

Tip

If you read one of these babies, you'll find some information that might turn out to be pretty helpful.

Use the following conventions (features) to help you work through the lessons:

On-screen text	Text that appears on-screen appears in **bold**.
Menu, dialog box, and window names	The first letter of each menu, dialog box, or window name is capitalized.
What you type	The information you type is **bold**.
What you press	The keys you press (for key combinations or commands) appear in **bold**.
Selection letters	The selection letter of each command or option is **bold** (such as File).

Once you have installed Windows, you can read the lessons from start to finish, or you can skip around from lesson to lesson. I'm not very picky about the way you use this book. I only ask one thing: that you don't take Windows *too* seriously. Take off your shoes, loosen your collar, and relax. Comfy? Okay, let's dig in . . .

Lesson 1

How Do I Start Windows?

Opening Your Windows

This is the easiest part of using Windows. First, make sure your computer and monitor are on. If you are at the C prompt (it looks like **C:>** or some similar variation), you are ready to start. Simply type **WIN** and press **Enter**. That's it.

Hey, This Doesn't Work If you type **WIN** and get a message like **Bad command or file name**, Windows might not be installed on your computer. Refer to the appendix in the back of this book to figure out how to install Windows. If you know that Windows is installed, make sure you are in the right directory. You might have to change to the Windows directory by typing **CD\ WINDOWS**.

Once you have successfully started Windows, the Windows Title screen briefly appears. You don't get to do anything while this screen is showing, you just have to look at it. Next, the opening screen appears (see Figure 1.1).

How Windows Is Set Up

Your first real look at Windows is, surprisingly enough, a window. Not just any window, mind you, but the *Program Manager* window. The Program Manager is the heart of all Windows operations. Everything you do from now on starts with Program Manager.

Because there are so many options to choose from at this point, everything is organized into *groups*.

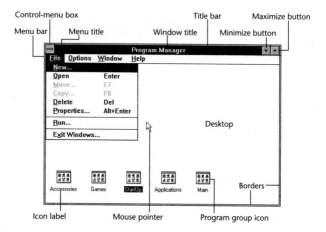

Figure 1.1   The Program Manager window with the File menu opened.

A Program Manager group is nothing more than a window containing a bunch of stuff that is somehow related. The *group icons* are the little graphics inside the Program Manager window that represent different groups. When you open a group icon, you will see another window with more icons in it. The icons inside a group window are called program-item icons. They represent applications or programs.

It's sort of like the drawers in your refrigerator. Vegetables go in the vegetable crisper, meat goes in the meat keeper, butter goes in the butter compartment, and so on. When you want to find say, a rutabaga, you look in the vegetable crisper. In Program Manager, if you want to find an application, you look in the Application group window.

As you can see in Figure 1.1, there is more to the Program Manager window than just icons. The parts you see in the figure are used throughout Windows and Windows applications to make it easier for you to get your work done. The theory is that if you learn how to use one window, you've learned how to use any window. The first step, then, is to learn about each part of the window. Have a look at them:

Border   Identifies the edge of the window.

Window title   Identifies the window and (often) suggests the use of the window.

Title bar   Gives added information, such as a document name, if you are working with a document in the window.

Desktop   This is the area outside the windows.

Mouse pointer   The pointer (usually an arrow) on-screen that lets you to select items and choose commands. You select items by moving the mouse pointer to the thing you want to select and *clicking* the mouse button. (Clicking just means to press the mouse button once quickly.)

Minimize and Maximize buttons   Click on these buttons to make the active window smaller or larger. Once the window is full-screen size, a button called the *Restore button* allows you to restore the window to its previous (smaller) size.

Icon   The Program Manager uses two types of icons, *group icons* and *program-item* icons. There are many other types of icons used throughout Windows and Windows applications.

Control-menu box   Used to access the Control menu, which contains handy commands for changing the size of the window, closing a window, and switching to another window.

Menu bar Displays the menu titles you can choose from. Each application might have different menu titles, but you open the menus the same way. Figure 1.1 shows the menu commands available in the File menu.

What Kind of Stuff Can I Do with Program Manager?

When you first install Windows, several groups are created automatically. (Remember, groups are just windows that contain related programs.) You don't even have to lift a finger (or a mouse). If you look in the Main group window, you'll find all sorts of fabulous tools. Here's what they are:

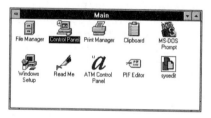

Figure 1.2 *This is what my Main group window looks like. Yours might look a little different.*

Control Panel An official-sounding tool that you can use to make Windows behave and appear exactly as you want it. You can change the colors of the screen or control the sensitivity of the mouse and keyboard.

File Manager This little tool is very important. You manage the files and directories on your disk.

You can use File Manager to do most of the same things you used to do at the (gasp) DOS prompt.

Print Manager   When you print a file in Windows, it doesn't actually go straight to the printer, it goes to the Print Manager. The Print Manager takes over the chore of sending the file to the printer so you don't get tied up in your application waiting for the thing to print.

Windows Setup   This lets you add things to Windows that were not included when Windows was installed. You use Setup to add applications to run in Windows.

Tutorial   This icon will only show up if you choose to include the Tutorial in the installation process. It's just a help feature.

PIF Editor   This is kind of a cool tool for people who have non-Windows applications running from Windows. The PIF files contain information that Windows uses to run non-Windows programs.

Clipboard Viewer   The Clipboard is the temporary storage area that holds data that you've cut or copied. The Clipboard Viewer is the tool you use to look at the Clipboard's contents.

MS-DOS Prompt   You can use this to jump out of Windows and get to the DOS prompt without actually exiting Windows. Why would anyone want to use DOS with File Manager just a few mouse clicks away, you ask? Beats me, but some die-hard DOS fans appreciate this feature.

Other program groups include Accessories (containing Write, Paintbrush, and other helpful tools), Games, StartUp, and Applications.

You've just learned how to open your Windows and you took a peek at the Program Manager. In the next lesson, you'll learn how to gallivant around with the mouse.

Lesson 2

Mousing Around

What's with This Mouse Thingy?

The mouse is the handy, little mechanism that sits by the side of your computer. Some extremely creative person noticed that this mechanism has a long "tail" (the cable that connects it to your computer) and is about the size of a small rodent; thus it was dubbed *mouse*. Mainly, you will use the mouse to select objects and choose commands.

Of course, you don't *have* to use the mouse. Sometimes it's easier than using the keyboard because you don't have to remember any keyboard commands. However, most mouse operations have keyboard equivalents, so you can use whichever one you want.

You'll see certain terms used throughout this chapter and through the rest of the book (such as *point, drag,* and *click*). You might as well become thoroughly familiar with these terms before skipping ahead into the really juicy Windows stuff.

How Do I Use This Thing?

First of all, get familiar with the way your mouse moves. Make little circles and squares with your mouse pointer to get comfortable with the speed and limitations of the mouse. Practice moving the mouse pointer to an icon or two. It takes a little bit of time to get used to moving the thing around, but pretty soon it will be a snap.

Now that we've gotten that pesky practice nonsense out of the way, let's use the mouse to perform some real commands. You'll often use the mouse to select icons and menu commands, so we'll start out with that. Selecting an object is a two-step process: first you point, and then you click.

Tip

Pointing means moving the mouse across your desk or mouse pad so the mouse cursor (usually a pointer) touches the object on-screen. You may have to pick up the mouse and reposition it if you run out of room on your desk.

Tip

Clicking means quickly pressing and releasing the left mouse button once. If the object is an icon or window, it will become highlighted (reverse color). If you click on a menu title, the menu will open.

Let's select Program Manager's File menu. First, point to the word File on the Menu bar, and then click the mouse. The menu will open, and you'll see all kinds of commands displayed. You can make the menu disappear by clicking anywhere outside the menu.

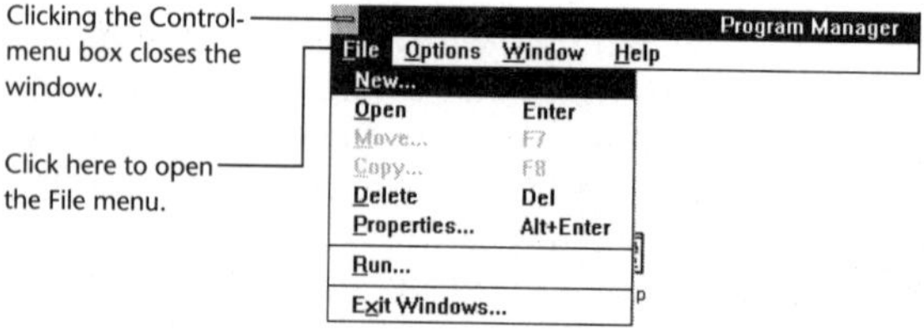

Clicking the Control-menu box closes the window.

Click here to open the File menu.

Program Manager
File Options Window Help
New...
Open   Enter
Move...   F7
Copy...   F8
Delete   Del
Properties... Alt+Enter
Run...
Exit Windows...

Figure 2.1 I clicked on the word File to get this menu.

Do You Feel a Draft?
(Opening and Closing Windows)

Using the mouse to open group icons or program-item icons is usually easier than using the keyboard. All you do is point to the icon you want to open and click the mouse button twice. This is called *double-clicking*, and you'll do it often in Windows. For example, double-clicking on a window's control box is a shortcut to closing a window. (The control box is that little square in the upper left corner of a window that looks like it has a hyphen in it.)

Open the Accessories group into a window by double-clicking on its icon. See how easy that was? To close it, you can double-click on the Control-menu box, or you can open the File menu and click on the Close command. Windows isn't choosy; you can do either one to achieve the same end.

Why Is It Telling Me That I'm Going to Exit Windows? If you've been double-clicking on Program Manager's Control-menu box, a little box will appear, saying that you are about to exit Windows. If you meant to double-click on the Control-menu box, click on **OK** or press **Enter**. If not, click on **Cancel** to go back to Windows.

Moving Stuff Around On-Screen

You can also use the mouse to *drag* an object (usually a window, dialog box, or icon) to a new position on-screen. Dragging means that you point to the thing you want to move, hold down the left mouse button (this is different from clicking), and then move the mouse pointer to the new location. The object you pointed to should move across the screen right along with the mouse pointer. When you release the mouse button, the object is dropped into place. (This process is usually called *drag and drop*, for obvious reasons.)

Remodeling Your Screen: Resizing a Window

Say one particular window is hogging so much screen space that you can't see the other windows. You have two choices: you can close the humongous window or you can *resize* it and make it smaller.

All you have to do is drag the window border to a new position. That changes the size of the window. Pretend Program Manager's window is getting obnoxious and unruly and you need to cut it down to size. You can make it smaller by pointing at the right-hand border of the window, holding down the left mouse button, and dragging the border to the left. When you release the mouse button, Shazam! The window is smaller.

Notice how the mouse pointer changed to a double-headed arrow when you pointed to the window border? That's just Windows way of telling you that the mouse pointer is in the right position to change the window size. As you become more familiar with Windows and Windows applications, you will learn that the mouse pointer changes a lot, and the shape of it tells you different things.

If you changed the right side of the border of Program Manager's window in the preceding example, you'll see that none of the other border sides were affected. You can change more than one border at once by using the border corner in the lower right corner of the Program Manager window. When you point to it and hold the left mouse button down, the pointer changes to a diagonal, double-headed arrow. Drag the border up and to the right, and you'll see two border sides of your window change position. When the window is the size you want, release the mouse button.

More Mouse Fun: Using Scroll Bars

When a window takes up more space than the area shown, *scroll bars* magically appear. You can use these things to move up, down, left, or right in a window. The only rule is that you have to use the mouse to use scroll bars.

Look at Figure 2.2 for an example. If you drag the Applications icon outside the lower right of the Program Manager window area and release the mouse button, scroll bars immediately appear. To use the scroll bars to view the icon, point at the down arrow located on the bottom of the vertical scroll bar. Click on the arrow and the window's contents scroll up. If you click on the scroll arrow on the right side of the horizontal scroll bar, the window's contents move left.

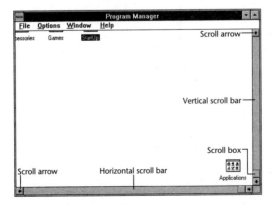

Figure 2.2 *Scroll bars provide handy ways to move around the screen.*

You can also drag the *scroll box* to move quickly to a distant area (top or bottom) of the window, kind of like an elevator. All you have to do is point to the scroll box in the scroll bar and hold down the mouse button, and then drag the scroll box to the new location. Release the mouse button when you think you've got the scroll box where you want it.

Window by Window   You can move the contents of a window one windowful at a time. To do so, just click in the *scroll bar* on either side of the scroll box.

You have just learned all about your mouse and how to use it to make Windows do what you want. Now, you'll learn how to use the keyboard to do all the same things.

Lesson 3

The Keyboard Bypass

Why Would I Want to Use the Keyboard When I Already Bought a Mouse?

There is no cut-and-dried way to use your computer. You might find that using the mouse is more efficient; you might prefer to use the keyboard to move around and select commands. Many people find that it's easier to use the mouse when moving around the screen and selecting things, but sometimes it's faster to select commands with the keyboard. I use a combination of the mouse and the keyboard, as you probably will when you get more familiar with some of the keyboard commands and even (oh, my!) memorize a few.

How is the keyboard more efficient than using the mouse, you ask? Well, there are certain *key combinations* that are called *shortcut keys*. A key combination is simply a couple of keys that you press at the same time. For example, to open Program Manager's File menu, you press **Alt+F**. This means you hold down the **Alternative** key while pressing the F key. Simple enough. The **Alt+F** key combination is considered a "shortcut" because you can just press two keys instead of moving your mouse up to the File menu and clicking on it.

Pretend you are typing a letter. It doesn't matter who the letter is to, it could be to anyone, even me. Since your hands are already on the keyboard, it would be faster for you just to press **Alt+F** to open the File menu than it would be to reach all the way over to the mouse and move it to the File menu and click, wouldn't it? Plus if you use the mouse, then you have to get your hands back on to the keyboard and worry about the whole home row thing. So in some cases, using the keyboard's shortcut keys can be a very handy way to navigate through windows and applications.

Keyboard Acrobatics

Of course, you can do other things with the keyboard besides pressing shortcut keys day in and day out. You can select icons and open applications the same as you can with the mouse. To move to a group icon in the Program Manager window, press **Ctrl+Tab** (this is another one of those crazy key combinations) as needed until the group icon you want is highlighted.

If you want to open the group whose icon you just highlighted, press **Enter**. The group icon opens into a window, like in Figure 3.1.

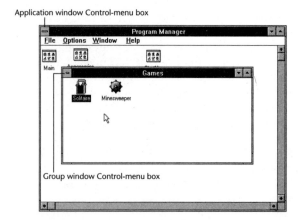

Figure 3.1 *I moved to the Games group icon and pressed* ***Enter*** *and this is what happened.*

When the group icon is opened into a window, you can just use the arrow keys to move between icons. That kooky Ctrl+Tab thing was only for windows that house group icons. If you want to open one of these program-item icons, press **Enter** when you've highlighted the right one.

What Does It Mean When It's Highlighted? The *active* icon (or window) is the one with the highlighted label (or title bar). Any commands you choose will affect the active window or icon. I'll be referring to "the active window" or "the active file" throughout the rest of the book, so it's a good thing you read this tip.

I Don't Want This Window on My Screen Any More

To close the window with the keyboard, press **Alt+hyphen** to open the Control menu (for group or file windows). If the window is an application window (such as Word for Windows or Excel), use **Alt+Spacebar** to open the Control menu. When the menu is open, press C to choose the Close command.

I Just Know I'll Forget Which One to Use Never fear, I have come up with an easy way to remember when to use the Alt+hyphen command and when to use the Alt+Spacebar command. Look at the bar in the Control-menu box. If it's a long bar, use the Spacebar (it's long); if it's short, use the hyphen (it's short). If you're having trouble locating the Control-menu box, look at Figure 3.1. I labeled it for you.

An even faster way to close a window with the keyboard is to press **Ctrl+F4** (if it's a group or file window) or **Alt+F4** (if it's an application window). I even have a trick for remembering the difference here: Alt goes with application. They both start with *A*'s.

Remodeling Windows with the Keyboard

You can also use the keyboard to move and resize windows. These operations can be performed more quickly using the mouse, but you have more control using the keyboard. It's your call.

To use the keyboard to move a window to a new location on the screen, open the window's Control menu, and then press **M** to choose the Move command. The mouse pointer will turn into a four-headed arrow (see Figure 3.2) positioned over the title bar. You can use the arrow keys to move the window to a new location, and then press **Enter** to accept the new location. If you want to cancel the operation and return the window to its original location, press **Esc**.

Why Can't I Choose Some of These Commands?
If a command is gray instead of black, you can't choose it. The Control menu **M**ove and **S**ize commands will not be active if the window is *maximized* (this means it fills up the whole screen). The **S**ize command is also unavailable if the window is *minimized* (this means the window is reduced to a mere icon).

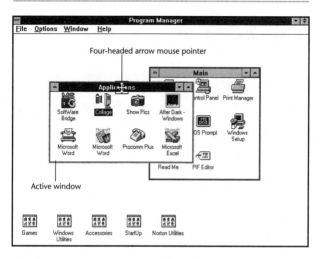

Figure 3.2 *Moving a window using the keyboard.*

To resize a window using the keyboard, open the window's Control menu, and press **S** to choose the Size command. The mouse pointer will turn into a four-headed arrow. You can use the arrow keys to move the mouse pointer to the border or corner of the window you want to resize. For example, if you press the right arrow key first, you will be able to resize the right border of the window. The four-headed arrow will become a two-headed arrow, indicating the directions you can move the border. Use the arrow keys to resize the window, and then press **Enter** to accept the new window size. **Esc** cancels the operation and returns the window to its original size.

Consider yourself armed with navigational savvy; you're done with this lesson. (Hopefully, you also picked up a couple of tricks to keep up your sleeve.) Turn the page to learn about very fun things called menus.

Lesson 4

Ordering from the Menu

What Are These Menus I've Been Hearing So Much About?

A *menu* is a group of related commands. Think of menus as categories: they are organized in logical groups. For example, from the Program Manager window, all the commands related to files may be found in the File menu. If every command on every menu was scattered all over the screen, you'd have a tough time trying to find the one you want. Menus are Windows way of keeping commands neatly organized for you. The names of the menus available appear in the menu bar.

Menu Commands Versus Shortcut Keys

When you first get started, you'll probably want to view the menus and select commands. Once you become more familiar with Windows, you'll be able to use *shortcut keys* for often-used commands. (Remember shortcut keys from the last lesson?) Shortcut keys typically combine the Alt, Ctrl, or Shift key with a function key (such as F1). If a shortcut key is available, it will be listed on the menu to the right of the command.

For example, Figure 4.1 shows the File menu from the Program Manager. You can choose File Properties to view the properties of a group or program-item icon, or press the shortcut key **Alt+Enter** to bypass the File menu.

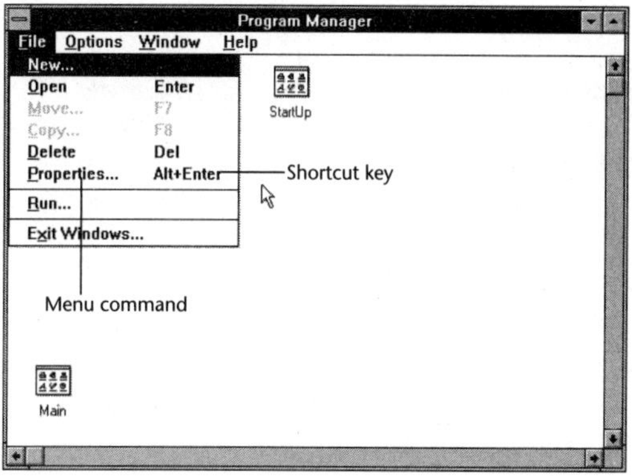

Figure 4.1   The Program Manager File menu.

What Does File Properties Mean? This book
uses the format *menu title, menu command* to tell you
what menu commands to choose. In the preceding
example, choosing **F**ile **P**roperties is equivalent to
opening the **F**ile menu and selecting the **P**roperties
command.

Reading a Menu

Common conventions (features) are used throughout
Windows menus. Figure 4.2 illustrates the Program
Manager File menu. Selection letters (letters you press
to choose a command) are underlined. Also, shortcut
keys (where available) are listed to the right of the
command. Use these to bypass menus.

Why Can't I Choose This Command? Some commands may appear grayed-out. That means that the command can only be used under certain circumstances, and those certain circumstances are not currently happening.

Another menu convention shown in Figure 4.2 is the use of the ellipsis (the three dot thing) after a command. The ellipsis tells you that as soon as you select the command, a *dialog box* will appear. These little boxes will creep up on you whenever Windows decides that it can't perform a command without more information from you. For more on dialog boxes, see Lesson 5.

Figure 4.2 The Program Manager File menu.

For example, suppose you want to exit Windows. You would open the File menu and then choose Exit Windows. (Notice the ellipsis?) A dialog box will appear, and you can click on **OK** or press **Enter** to exit Windows. If you don't want to exit Windows and were just following along for kicks, click on the **Cancel** button, or press **Esc**. You should be right back where you started.

Another common menu symbol is the check mark. The check mark indicates that a menu option is currently active. Each time you choose the menu command, the option is turned on or off (like a light switch).

Choosing Menu Commands with the Mouse

To select a menu with the mouse, click on the menu title in the menu bar. The menu opens to display the available commands. To choose a particular command, click on it with the mouse pointer.

Here's an example. To see the **Help** options available for the Program Manager, just click on the **Help** menu title in the Program Manager menu bar (see Figure 4.3). (*Remember*, to close this or any window, double-click on the **Control-menu** box.)

Figure 4.3   *The Help menu.*

Choosing Menu Commands Using the Keyboard

You can also select menus with the keyboard. Press **Alt** to activate the menu bar of the active window. Notice that the first menu title becomes highlighted. Once the menu bar is active, you can choose between two methods to select a menu:

☞ Use the arrow keys to highlight the menu title you want and press **Enter**.

☞ Press the underlined letter of the menu item. (For example, to open the Help menu, you would press **H**.)

To open the Control-menu with the keyboard, press **Alt+Spacebar** if the window is an application window (such as Microsoft Word for Windows or Program Manager) or **Alt+hyphen** if the window is a document or group window. To choose a command from the menu, highlight your selection using the arrow keys and then press **Enter**, or you can press the underlined letter of the command.

Commands, Options, or Selections? Commands, menu options, and menu selections all refer to the same thing—the stuff that you choose from a menu. To add to the confusion, commands may be performed, executed, or selected. All this jibber-jabber simply means that the computer carries out the instructions associated with the command when you select it.

To close the Control menu (or any menu for that matter), press **Esc**.

Now that you can use menus, you can interpret what's in them. In the next lesson, you'll have even more fun (trust me) learning about dialog boxes.

Lesson 5

Chatting with Dialog Boxes

What's a Dialog Box?

Windows uses dialog boxes to force information out of you. When a dialog box appears, it means that you need to provide more information before an operation can be completed. A menu command followed by an ellipsis (...) indicates that a dialog box will spring up. Dialog boxes are also used to warn you about a problem or to confirm that something major is about to take place (for example, the Exit Windows dialog box).

Okay, So What's In a Dialog Box?

Dialog boxes vary in complexity. Some ask you to confirm an operation before it is executed, and all you have to do is select **OK** or **Cancel**. Other dialog boxes dig really deep, asking you to specify several options.

Here's what you might see in a typical dialog box:

Text Box A text box allows you to type in an entry, for example, a name for a file you want to save or a label for an icon you've just added to a group.

List Box A list box presents a list of possible choices from which you may choose. Scroll bars allow you to scroll through the list if it's long. Often, a text box is associated with a list box. The list item that you select appears in the text box associated with the list.

Drop-Down List Box   A single-line list box that opens to display a list of choices when you click on the down-arrow button on the right side of the list box.

Option Buttons   Option buttons present a group of related choices from which you may choose only one. Option buttons are sometimes incorrectly referred to as *radio buttons*. Some people call them radio buttons because they are like the buttons on old car radios: only one can be pushed in at a time. This phrase is less technical than "option buttons," and therefore deemed less accurate.

Check Boxes   Check boxes present a single option or group of related options. The command option is active if an X appears in the box next to it. You can pick as many of these as you want.

Command Buttons   Command buttons carry out the command displayed on the button (Open, Quit, Cancel, OK, and so on). If there is an ellipsis on the button, choosing it will open another dialog box (Options).

To move the cursor around to different sections of the dialog box with the keyboard, use the **Tab** key. Once a particular section is highlighted, you can use the arrow keys to select options. For example, say the dialog box in Figure 5.1 is on your screen, and you want to select the calc.exe file instead of the cardfile.exe file. Press **Tab** until the cursor is in the File Name section, and then use the arrow keys to highlight the **calc.exe** file. When highlighted, it should appear in the text box above the list box.

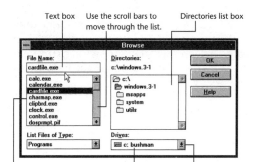

Figure 5.1 *This is a typical dialog box.*

Tip

I Hate Pressing Tab If, for some reason, you just can't bring yourself to press **Tab** to move around the dialog box, you can hold down the **Alt** key while pressing the selection letter of the section you want to go to. For example, to go to the **D**irectories list box, press **Alt+D**. You can also use these handy shortcut keys to toggle (turn on and off) option buttons and check boxes. Nifty, eh?

Tip

Now What Have I Done? If you accidentally select the **Cancel** command button, don't worry. You can always go back to the dialog box and start over. Accidentally selecting **Cancel** is much better than accidentally selecting **OK** before you're ready. You could tell Windows to do all the wrong things if you blunder around and select **OK** too soon.

Let's pause for a moment to reflect upon those information-gathering things called dialog boxes. Okay, that's enough. Let's move on to the next lesson, where you will learn how to get help when you're stuck (no, you can't call me).

Lesson 6

Help Wanted

What to Do When There's Nowhere Else to Turn

If you're anything like me, there will be many times when you will need a helping hand when using Windows. The brilliant creators of Windows have foreseen this need and have provided an extensive on-line help system for the likes of you and me. No one can be expected to know everything about Windows (and I don't think anyone would want to), so when you are in a bind, remember this magic help key: **F1**.

In Windows and most Windows applications, you can press **F1** from virtually anywhere and the help system will automatically appear. Of course, you can also select the **Help** menu from the menu bar and choose commands from it, but pressing **F1** is quicker.

Many dialog boxes will have a **Help** button that you can choose instead of OK or Cancel. Selecting this button will bring up a window that contains specific information about the command you are trying to perform. Pretty handy, eh? This means that if you aren't sure of how to do something, you can at least start the command. When you get to the part when you don't have the faintest idea what to do next, choose the **Help** button.

To take a brief peek at what the **Help** menu has in store for you, check out Figure 6.1. It shows what you can do from the Help screen. If you're not sure what you're looking for, choose the Contents button. Windows will run through a list of topics that you can choose from.

Figure 6.1   The Help screen in all its glory.

If you know exactly what you want to find, choose the Search button. A dialog box like the one in Figure 6.2 will appear, and you can to type in or select the topic you want from a list box. When that's done, select the Show Topics button to see some subtopics. Choose the one you want, and then select the Go To button. The information will appear on the screen.

Figure 6.2   *Here's what you'll see if you select the Search button.*

One really cool thing about the Help system is that you can click on any of the words that are underlined and a window will automatically appear with information about that topic. Let's say you are looking at the screen in Figure 6.1 and you want to figure out how to quit Windows. You would move your mouse pointer so that it's right on the Quit Windows selection (See how the pointer changes to a hand?), and then click.

To get out of a Help window, you can click on the Close button or press **Esc**. To exit the Help system, select Exit from the File menu, or double-click on the **Control-menu** box.

And that's all there is to it! Now you can force Windows to help you when you're in a jam. Are you ready to learn how to exit Windows? Read on!

Lesson 7

When It's Time to Quit and Go Home

How Do I Get Out of This Program Manager Thing?

Like most other Windows commands, there are several ways to exit Windows. You can use Program Manager's File menu, the Control menu, or a shortcut key. The following sections go into a little more detail.

The Roundabout Way: Using the File Menu

You can exit Windows using the File menu if you want, but frankly, the other ways are faster. Here are some instructions just in case you want to know how to do it.

If you're using the mouse, click on the File menu, and then choose the Exit Windows command. A dialog box that says **This will end your Windows session** will appear (see Figure 7.1). Click on the **OK** button.

If you want to use the keyboard, first press **Alt+F** to open the File menu. Then select the Exit Windows command by pressing **X**, or by using the arrow keys to highlight the command, and then pressing **Enter**. When the Exit Windows dialog box appears, as shown in Figure 7.1, press **Enter** to select OK.

Figure 7.1   *The Exit Windows dialog box.*

A Quick Way to Exit Using the Control Menu

This is my favorite way to exit Windows: double-click on the Program Manager Control-menu box. It's easy and hassle free.

> **Can I Use the Keyboard to Exit Using the Control-menu Box?**   Of course you can. It's not faster than using the **F**ile menu, but you can do it this way if you want. Just press **Alt+Spacebar** to open Program Manager's Control menu, and then select the **C**lose command. When the dialog box pops up, select **OK**.

There's a Shortcut Key, Isn't There?

As you may have noticed if you looked in the Control menu, a shortcut key is available to exit Windows. Once you have closed any open documents and applications and returned to the Program Manager window, press **Alt+F4**.

Windows' Protection Plan

Because you can work with several documents and applications at one time, it's easy to get carried away and forget to save a document before you exit Windows. Fear not; Windows protects you. For example, if you're working on a document in the Write application and you try to exit Windows without saving the document, the dialog box shown in Figure 7.2 prompts you to save your changes.

Figure 7.2 *The Write: Save Current Changes? dialog box.*

You can just select Yes to save the changes, No to ignore Windows' warning, or **Cancel** to stop the exiting process. This dialog box helps you avoid losing document changes.

Uh-Oh, I Accidentally Pressed No! Tough luck, buster. This message is your only warning. If you accidentally respond **N**o to saving current changes, the changes made in the document are lost. If it's any consolation, everyone loses stuff because they forgot to save it at one time or another. I know, I know, that doesn't make you feel better, but at least you know you're not alone.

Even though Windows provides this protective dialog box, it would be a wise move to get in the habit of closing documents and applications yourself before quitting Windows. In most Windows applications, you can choose File Save to save a document.

You have painlessly learned how to exit Windows, and, hopefully, you memorized the valuable advice about saving your work before exiting (quiz on Friday). Now let's get into the nitty-gritty: how to start (and exit) applications.

Lesson 8

Getting In and Out of Applications

How Do I Start a Windows Application?

First of all, a Windows application is a program designed to take advantage of the *graphical user interface* built into Windows. Graphical user interface is just a fancy-schmancy way of saying that Windows programs look the same and generally use the same commands. By the way, the abbreviation for graphical user interface, GUI, is pronounced "GOO-ey." (I'm not joking, this is for real.)

Windows' GUI lets you start (and exit) most Windows applications using the same procedures. There are several ways to start a Windows application, but we'll only discuss two in this lesson.

What If I'm Not Using a Windows Application?
If you are using a DOS application through Windows, you will need to consult the manual for that application to learn how to start and exit.

Easy Street: Using the Application's Icon

You will probably most often use the program-item icon to start an application. When you installed the Windows application, a program-item icon for the application was added to a group in Program Manager. You might have to look around in Program Manager's groups to find that icon, but it's there. For example, if you want to use Write, Windows' word processing program, you would need to open the Accessories group icon. Figure 8.1 shows the Accessories group window and the icons you might see in it.

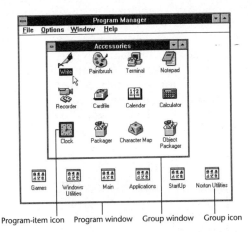

Program-item icon   Program window   Group window   Group icon

Figure 8.1   *Program-item icons in the Accessories group.*

If you're using the mouse, first double-click on the Program Manager group that contains the program-item icon for the application you want to use. Then double-click on the program-item icon for the application. The application window appears.

To start an application using the keyboard, press **Ctrl+Tab** to highlight the desired program group icon in Program Manager's window. After pressing **Enter** to open the group window, use the arrow keys to highlight the program-item icon for the application you want to use. Then press **Enter** to start the application.

The Hard Way: Using the Run Command

You can also use the Program Manager File Run command to start applications. You can use the **Run** command if you want to enter the command yourself or change the way the application is started. For example, most word processors can be started so that a file you specify is automatically opened and ready to edit. Figure 8.2 displays the command that will open WordPerfect for Windows (**wpwin**) with a file (**report.wpp**) open and ready to edit. If necessary, you can include the path statement (drive and directory) for the program file and/or the document file.

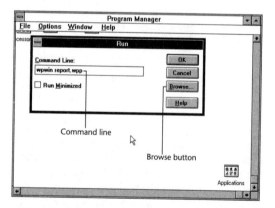

Figure 8.2 *Loading WordPerfect for Windows and a document file using the Windows File Run command.*

To use the **Run** command, choose File Run. When the Run dialog box appears, just type the command in the text box. When the command is complete, select **OK**. (If you decide not to use the **Run** command, select **Cancel**.)

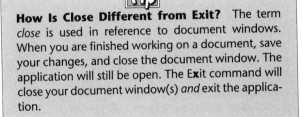

What If I Forgot the Command?   Suppose you don't remember the command that will run the application. The easiest thing to do is to use the **B**rowse button on the Run dialog box. When you select it, a dialog box appears that lets you see your files. You can pick the one you want from the list box.

Exiting Windows Applications

Let's say that you've been slaving away in an application for a few hours and now you're finished. You've saved and closed all the open documents, and you're ready to exit.

There are three ways to exit a Windows application: you can double-click on the **Control-menu** box, select the Exit command from the File menu, or press **Alt+F4**. It's almost exactly the same as exiting Windows.

How Is Close Different from Exit?   The term *close* is used in reference to document windows. When you are finished working on a document, save your changes, and close the document window. The application will still be open. The E**x**it command will close your document window(s) *and* exit the application.

You just learned how to start and exit applications. In the next lesson, I'll show you how to remodel your windows by resizing and moving them.

Lesson 9

Custom-Made Windows: Resizing and Moving

The Fabulous Maximize, Minimize, and Restore Commands

Sometimes, the size of a window is all wrong for what you are trying to do. It might not be big enough for you to see its full contents, or it might be so big that you can't see other windows. A good way to resize a window is to use the Maximize, Minimize, and Restore commands.

Minimizing a window means reducing it to an icon, not allowing you to see its contents. When you maximize a window, it takes up the whole screen and doesn't let you see any other windows. The Restore command and button will be available if your window is minimized or maximized. When you select it, your window will return to the size it was before you changed it.

If you use the mouse, you will use the Maximize, Minimize, and Restore buttons located on the right side of the window title bar. (Look at Figure 9.1 to see where they are.) If you are using a keyboard, you'll find the commands on the Control menu.

The window in Figure 9.1 is maximized to full-screen size. Notice that only the minimize and restore buttons are available in a maximized window.

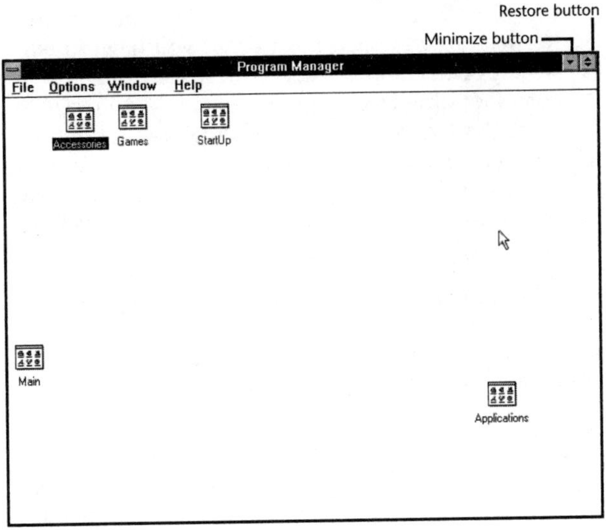

Restore button

Minimize button ——

Figure 9.1 The Program Manager window maximized to full-screen size.

Sizing Things Up

Sizing windows is easy with the mouse. You simply drag the window border to change the size of the window.

If you place the mouse pointer on the border you want to resize, the mouse pointer will change into one of the shapes displayed in Table 9.1. You can then drag the border to the new position. A faint line will show you where the new border will be. Release the mouse button when you've got it where you want it.

To resize a window using the keyboard, you have to open the window's Control menu, and then choose the Size command. The pointer becomes a four-headed arrow, which means that you have to tell it which of the four borders to resize by pressing the corresponding arrow key. For example, to resize the right border, press the right arrow key. The mouse pointer will transform into one of the shapes in Table 9.1. Use the arrow keys to resize the window. When the faint lines show the sizing you want, press **Enter**. To cancel the operation, press **Esc**.

Table 9.1	**Window Resizing Mouse Pointers**
Mouse Pointer	Description
⇕	The vertical double-headed arrow appears when you position the mouse pointer over either the top or bottom window border. It lets you resize the window by dragging the border up or down.
⇔	The horizontal double-headed arrow appears when you position the mouse pointer over either side of the window border. It allows you to resize the window by dragging the border left or right.

Mouse Pointer	Description
↖	The diagonal double-headed arrow appears when you position the mouse pointer over any of the four corners of the window border. It lets you resize the window by dragging the corner diagonally.

Tip

Hey, Where Did My Icons Go?   When you reduce the size of a window, some of the contents might not be visible in the resulting window size. Remember to use the scroll bars to see the contents of the window.

I Want This Window to Be Over There

When you start working with a bunch of windows, moving them around becomes as important as sizing them. You can move a window with the mouse or keyboard.

To move a window using the mouse, point at the Windows title bar and drag it to a new location. Simple enough. To use the keyboard, open the window's **Control** menu, and choose the **Move** command. The pointer will appear as a four-headed arrow. Use the arrow keys to move the window to a new location, and then press **Enter** when the window is in the right place. To cancel the operation and return the window to its original location, and press **Esc**.

Changing windows all around by resizing them and moving them has now been added to your Windows repertoire. Feel like cavorting around the desktop in multiple windows? Good, because that's what you'll learn next.

Lesson 10

A Plethora of Open Windows

Isn't One Window Enough?

Sometimes, using one window just isn't practical. With Windows you can use more than one application at a time, and because each Windows application supports multiple document windows, you can imagine the mind-boggling amount of windows that could be open at once. All this can make your desktop pretty congested! That's why it's important to be able to arrange and switch between windows easily.

You learned how to open a program item icon into a window by double-clicking on it; to open another window you simply double-click on another icon. To open a new document window within an application, choose the File New command associated with the application.

Window Arrangements

Once you have multiple open windows, you can use the commands under the Window menu to arrange the windows. Figure 10.1 shows several windows open at the same time. (Yow, what a mess!) These windows desperately need to be arranged.

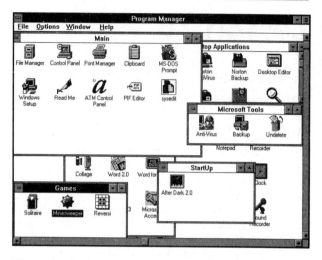

Figure 10.1 *A very messy Program Manager with multiple windows open.*

Cascading Windows

A good way to get control of a confusing desktop is to choose the Window Cascade command. Cascade is just what is sounds like: windows flowing over the top of each other. When you choose this command, the title bar of each window is visible. Look at Figure 10.2 for an example.

Cascade Quickly Press the shortcut key combination **Shift+F5** to cascade your windows without using the **W**indow menu.

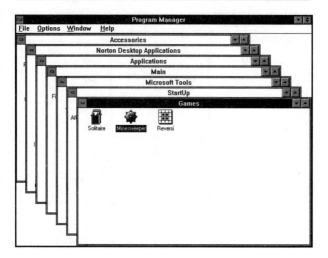

Figure 10.2 *The windows after selecting Window Cascade.*

But I Want to See What's in My Windows

You can choose the Window Tile command if you want to see the contents of several windows at once. When you choose this command, Windows resizes and moves each open window so they appear side-by-side. Look at Figure 10.3 for an example.

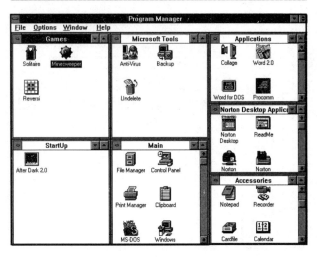

Figure 10.3   The windows after selecting Window Tile.

Timely Tiling   Press the shortcut key combination **Shift+F4** to tile your windows without using the **W**indow menu.

My Icons Are a Mess

Another Window command is Arrange Icons. This command is handy after you move icons out of your way by dragging them with the mouse. When things get confusing, choose Window Arrange Icons to clean up after yourself.

Can I Get There from Here?

Another common dilemma when using multiple windows is how to move between windows. The application (and document window, if applicable) currently in use has a highlighted title bar. That's how you know which window is active.

Where Am I? The window currently in use is called the *active* window. Moving to a new window means you are changing the window that is active.

If you are using a mouse, click on any part of the window you want to use (make active). The title bar is highlighted, and you may work in the window.

To use the keyboard, open the **W**indow menu by pressing **Alt+W**. Figure 10.4 shows the Program Manager's **W**indow menu. Notice that the available windows appear in a numbered list. Simply press the number next to the window title you want to activate. Most Windows applications make use of the **W**indow menu.

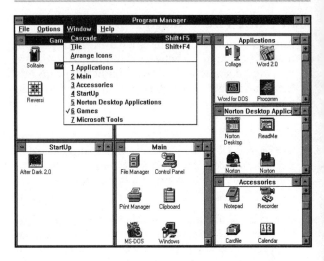

Figure 10.4   The Program Manager's Window menu.

How Do I Get to Another Application?

Remember that Windows allows you to have multiple windows open within an application *and* have multiple applications open at the same time. You already know how to move between windows in the same application, and now you'll learn how to move between applications.

Using the Task List

A dialog box called the Task List can be used to switch between applications. A sample Task List is shown in Figure 10.5. There are three applications running. Notice that the entry for Write (Windows word processor application) is followed by the name of the active document window (RPT2.WRI).

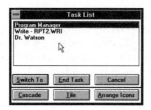

Figure 10.5 *The Task List with three running applications.*

To use the mouse to switch applications using the Task List, first click on the **Control-menu** box. Click on the Switch To command and the Task List appears. Highlight the application to switch to by clicking on it. Click on the **S**witch To button, and you are whisked away to the application.

The keyboard can also be used with the Task List. Press **Ctrl+Esc** to display the Task List. Use the arrow keys to highlight the application you want, and then press **Enter**.

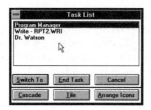

What If I Don't Want to Use the Task List?
Hold down the **Alt** key, and press the **Tab** key. A dialog box appears displaying the name of one of the open applications. Each time you press the **Tab** key, a new (open) application is displayed. When you see the application you want, release the **Alt** key and you will switch to that application. If you decide you don't want to switch task after all, press **Esc**, and release the **Alt** key. This technique works with both Windows and non-Windows applications.

In this lesson, you learned how to control your unruly desktop by opening and arranging multiple windows. Step this way and I'll show you how to move information between windows with the amazing Cut, Copy, and Paste commands.

Lesson 11

Hey, How Do I Print This Masterpiece?

What Is the Print Manager, Anyway?

You can't print anything without the Print Manager. It acts as the middleman between your printer and the application you are printing from. When you choose File Print from most Windows applications, the font and file information is handed off to the Print Manager. The Print Manager then feeds the information to the printer. This allows you to continue working in your application while your job is printed.

What's a Print Job? A *print job* (or simply *job*) is created when you choose the **P**rint command from the application in which you are working. It's just the thing you are trying to print.

How Does the Print Manager Keep Track of the Print Jobs?

When you print a document, the printer usually begins processing the job immediately. What happens if the printer is already working on another job, you ask? Well, the Print Manager acts as a *print queue* and holds the job until the printer is ready for it.

What's a Queue? Here's some trivia for you: A British friend would say he had to "queue" up at the bus stop instead of "line" up at the bus stop. Think of the print queue as the same thing: it's the place where all the print jobs wait in line for their turn.

Figure 11.1 illustrates the document SLIME.DOC in the print queue. As you can see, the percent of the document that has been printed is shown (15% of 13K) along with the time and date the document was sent to print. Notice also that the printer is shown to be printing. This tells you that the document was just sent to the queue and is beginning to print.

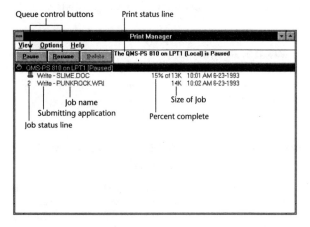

Figure 11.1 *The Print Manager print queue window.*

To display the print queue, open the **Main** group icon from the Program Manager. Open the **Print Manager** icon (see Figure 11.1). The Print Manager window appears with a list of queued documents. If no documents are waiting to print, a message tells you the printer is idle.

Can I Control the Print Jobs Myself?

Once they are in the queue, you can change the order in which the jobs print, pause and resume a print job, or delete a job before it prints.

Reordering Jobs in the Queue

To use the mouse to change the order of a job in the queue, drag the job entry to a new position in the list. If you're using the keyboard, first use the arrow keys to highlight the document that you want to reposition. Then hold down **Ctrl**, and use the arrow keys to move the job to the new position in the queue. Release the **Ctrl** key when you're done.

First Come, First Served You cannot reorder or place a job before the job that is currently printing.

Pausing and Resuming the Print Queue

You may want to pause the queue and then resume printing later. For example, the paper in the printer may be misaligned. Pausing the print queue will give you time to correct the problem.

To pause the print queue, select the **Pause** button, or press **Alt+P** while in the Print Manager window. To resume printing, select the **Resume** button, or press **Alt+R**.

It Says My Printer Is Stalled This might happen while the printer is processing your print job. If it does, **stalled** will appear in the printer status line. Press **Alt+R** to start printing again. Chances are that a problem somewhere along the line caused the printer to stall. This means the queue will stall again, and you will have to solve the problem. Refer to your printer's documentation for help.

Deleting a Print Job

Sometimes, you'll send a document to be printed and then change your mind. For example, you may think of other text to add to the document or realize you forgot to spell check your work. In such a case, deleting the print job is easy.

From the Print Manager window, select the job to delete. Select the Delete button or press **Alt+D**. A message will appear for you to confirm the deletion. Select **OK**.

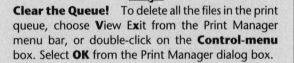

Clear the Queue! To delete all the files in the print queue, choose **V**iew E**x**it from the Print Manager menu bar, or double-click on the **Control-menu** box. Select **OK** from the Print Manager dialog box.

Piece of cake! You can now print out your material and show your friends that you really have been working and not just playing Solitaire. In the next lesson, you will learn how to use the scary-sounding Control Panel.

Lesson 12

I'll Do It My Way: Using the Control Panel

I Don't Think I Like the Control Panel

Don't be intimidated by the official-sounding Control Panel. Once you start using it, you'll find out that it's pretty friendly. *Control Panel* is just a phrase that someone chose to describe this application. Found in the Main group window, it enables you to control many aspects of Windows (see Figure 12.1). We'll talk about some of those aspects in this lesson:

- ☛ Changing colors on your desktop
- ☛ Changing the date and time
- ☛ Changing your mouse's behavior
- ☛ Changing the way your keyboard reacts

Figure 12.1   The Windows Control Panel.

They Could Have Chosen Something Better Than Drab Gray

Fortunately, you can change the color of many components of Windows with the Control Panel. Not only can you customize your desktop by choosing your own colors, you might learn to use Windows faster if you associate certain elements with certain colors. You could look for a particular color *and* shape, instead of just a shape.

Enough stalling, let's change some colors. First, open the Control Panel. (It's in Program Manager's Main group.) Then, open the **Color** program-item. In the dialog box that appears, open the Schemes drop-down list box by clicking on the down arrow button or pressing **Alt+↓**. You'll see a list of different color schemes like the one in Figure 12.2. When you select one with your arrow keys and press **Enter**, the colors in the sample window change to show you what the scheme looks like. When you've found the one you want, select **OK**.

Current color scheme

Sample of current color scheme

Select to access color palette

Figure 12.2 *The Black Leather Jacket Color Scheme selected on the Color dialog box.*

This Needs a Little More Yellow   Feeling artsy? After you become more comfortable with Windows, you can create your own color scheme. From the Color dialog box, select the Color **P**alette button. A new section of the Color dialog box will allow you to assign different colors to the various Windows components (title bar, buttons, menus, and so on). You can then save your creation as your very own color scheme. Magnifique!

I Thought the Date and Time Were Automatically Correct

The date and time are usually correct. But if the power goes out or if your computer just goes wacky for whatever reason, sometimes the date and time get messed up. The system date and time are stamped into files as they are created or modified so you'll know when you last worked on them. It's important to always make sure the date and time are right.

To check or set the date and time, open the **Date/ Time** icon from the Control Panel. In the dialog box that appears, use the **Tab** key or the mouse to move between digits in the date and time. Then just enter the appropriate numbers. (If you just have to use the mouse to enter numbers, you can click on the portion of the date or time you want to change and click on the up or down arrow button to increase or decrease the value. Some people always have to be difficult.) Select **OK** or press **Enter** to accept the changes you have made.

My Mouse Is Acting Funny

You can modify the settings for your mouse by selecting the **Mouse** icon in the Control Panel and using your finely honed dialog box maneuvering skills to select options in the dialog box. You can change:

- ☞ The speed of mouse tracking (how fast and far the pointer moves when you move the mouse).

- ☞ The speed of the double-click (the time allowed between the first and second click so that your action is recognized as a double-click and not just two single clicks).

- ☞ The use of the left and right buttons (can be swapped for you lefties out there).

- ☞ A trail of mouse pointers that follow the pointer movement. (By turning the trail on, you can drive an unsuspecting user up the wall.)

> **Try It, You'll Like It**   Always use the **T**est area to try new settings before leaving the screen. For example, if you set the **D**ouble-Click Speed all the way to Fast, you may not be able to double-click fast enough for it to register.

Hey! My Keyboard Is Acting Funny

You can change how long it takes for a key to be repeated and how fast a key repeats when it is held down. Use the dialog box that appears when you select the **Keyboard** icon from the Control Panel to make these changes. Make sure to test the new settings out in the Test area.

Now that you've learned all about customizing your desktop and you've got everything arranged exactly as you want it, let's move on. In the next lesson, you'll learn about drives and directories, which is much more fascinating than it sounds.

Lesson 13

Directing Your Drives and Driving Your Directories

What Are Drives?

Under the hood of most computers these days you'll find a hard drive and one or two floppy disk drives. Simply put, the *drive* is the thing that makes a disk work. Disks and drives are like cassette tapes and tape players. One doesn't do you much good unless you've got the other.

Each drive is given a letter name. On most computers, *A* and *B* are floppy disk drives, used to store and retrieve data from floppy diskettes. The hard drive (the permanent drive that's inside your computer) is typically drive C. If the computer has more than one hard disk, or if the hard disk has been divided into multiple partitions, or *logical drives*, the additional drives are usually labeled D, E, F, and so on. (If you don't know what partitions are, you probably don't have them, so don't worry about them.)

You Say Tom-a-to, I Say To-mah-to   Ever wonder why some people call it a *hard disk* and others call it a *hard drive*? Well, the truth is that both are essentially correct. Since hard disks and their drives are not easily separated, the terms *disk* and *drive* are often used interchangeably when referring to hard disks.

What Are Directories?

Because you can cram so much data onto a hard disk, they are usually divided into *directories*. Directories can help you keep data organized. For example, drive C typically has a separate directory for DOS (the Disk Operating System), a directory for Windows, and so on. Floppy disks can contain directories too, but usually don't. (Because of their limited capacity, it is easy to keep track of files on a floppy disk without using directories.)

Disk space is not set aside for individual directories; in fact, directories take up hardly any disk space at all. If you think of a disk as a file drawer full of papers, directories are like tabbed folders used to organize the papers into manageable groups.

What Are Files?

Directories hold files, just as folders hold pieces of paper. A file may contain the instructions for the computer to perform (typically called *program* or *executable files*). Or a file may contain a text document that you can read (often referred to as a *document file*).

Regardless of the type of file, its directory or drive, you can use Windows' *File Manager* to view and control the little rascals.

What the Heck Is the File Manager and How Do I Start It?

The File Manager is a really nifty Windows program that you can use instead of using DOS. (DOS is that very nasty ogre of an operating system that expects you to type in arcane commands when you want it to do something.) File Manager is much prettier than DOS, and it's easy to manipulate your files with it.

To start the File Manager, just open the File Manager program-item icon from Program Manager's Main group. Figure 13.1 shows the File Manager window. The directory window's title bar shows the drive for the information displayed (in this case, drive C).

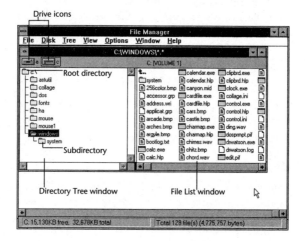

Figure 13.1 *The File Manager window displaying a directory window.*

How Are All My Directories Arranged?

Look at Figure 13.1 again. See how the left side of the directory window kind of looks like a tree? (Okay, so it doesn't really look like a tree. Try to use your imagination.) People call this representation of directories and subdirectories a *directory tree* because it branches out like a regular tree. (The directory tree on your screen will probably contain different directories from the one shown in the figure.)

In Figure 13.1, you can see that my drive C contains a directory called *windows*. The *windows* directory has a subdirectory: *system*. Since my *windows* directory is highlighted, the right side of the screen contains a list of the files in the *windows* directory. Did you notice that the folder icon next to the highlighted directory appears as an open folder? Pretty cool, huh?

How Do I Change Directories?

Since the file list changes every time you highlight a new directory, you can look at the contents of a whole bunch of directories in no time at all. You can point to the directory you want and click, or you can use the keyboard to move to it. Check out Table 13.1 to figure out which key you should use.

Table 13.1 Keys to Change the Directory

Use This Key	To Change To
↑	The directory above the selected one.
↓	The directory below the selected one.
←	The subdirectory under the selected one.
→	The directory at the next higher level than the selected one.
Ctrl+↑	The previous directory at the same level.
Ctrl+↓	The next directory at the same level.

Use This Key	To Change To
Home	The root directory.
End	The last directory in the tree.
First letter of name	Any specific directory.

What's a Root Directory?   To continue with the whole tree analogy, the root directory is the one at the base of the tree. In Windows, directory trees grow upside down. The root directory appears at the top of the File Manager window, and all other directories branch off below the root directory. In Figure 13.1, the root directory is shown as C:\.

What's a Subdirectory?   Any directory can have a *subdirectory*. You can think of it as having file folders within file folders; they help you organize your files. In Figure 13.1, *system* is a subdirectory of *windows*. You can have subdirectories of subdirectories if you want, but don't get too carried away with them.

How Do I Get to My Subdirectories?

As you noticed before, the directory tree shows the subdirectory of the **windows** directory (*system*). You can *collapse* (decrease the detail of) the directory tree, so that the subdirectory does not appear. You can also *expand* (increase the detail of) the directory tree, so that subdirectories many levels deep will *all* show.

Table 13.2 lists methods used to expand or collapse
the directory levels.

**Table 13.2 Methods of Expanding
or Collapsing Directory
Levels**

Activity	Action
Expand with the mouse	Double-click on the directory icon.
Expand with the keyboard	Use the arrow keys to select the directory, and press + (plus).
Collapse with the mouse	Double-click on the directory icon.
Collapse with the keyboard	Use the arrow keys to select the directory and press - (hyphen).

That's Not Fast Enough Use the File Manager
Tree menu to speed expanding and collapsing of
multiple directories. Select **T**ree Expand **B**ranch to
expand all levels for the selected directory. Select **T**ree
Expand **A**ll to expand the entire tree. Select **T**ree
Collapse **B**ranch to collapse the levels for the selected
directory.

> **It's Only for Show**   Collapsing and expanding affects only the display; it doesn't alter your directories in any way. Rest assured, your directories were not deleted when you collapsed them.

How Do I Change Drives?

You can change drives to see the directories and files contained on a different disk. To change drives with the mouse, click on the drive icon in the upper left corner of the Directory Tree window. To use the keyboard, press **Ctrl+*drive letter*** (for example, press **Ctrl+A** for drive A).

How Do I Get Out of This Crazy Thing?

Each directory window can be minimized and maximized within File Manager, or closed altogether. (You learned about minimizing and maximizing in Lesson 9.) If you have more than one directory window open at once, you might want to minimize all but the one you're working with.

You can also minimize or close the File Manager window to return to the Program Manager. If you're not going to use File Manager again right away, it is better to close it rather than minimize it, to conserve system resources.

To close the File Manager, double-click on the Control-menu box or press **Alt+F** (for File), and then X (for Exit).

You just learned how to view the contents of disks and directories using the very cool File Manager. Now, let's learn how to create and delete those pesky things called directories.

Lesson 14

The Frankenstein Directory: You Made It, You Can Destroy It

Why Would I Want to Create a Directory?

There are several reasons you might want to create a directory. A common reason to create a directory is to store document files. For example, you may want to create a directory to store documents you create with the Write application. That way, the document files will not be scattered among the more than a hundred Windows program files in the Windows directory. Having a separate directory for Write documents can make it much easier to find the documents you've created.

To create a directory, first open the **File Manager**. Highlight the directory you want the new directory to reside under. (The directory you create will be a subdirectory of the directory you highlight.) If you don't want the new directory to be a subdirectory of another directory, highlight the root directory (**C:**).

After you've taken care of that highlighting business, Choose File Create Directory. In the Create Directory dialog box that appears, type the Name of the new directory, (up to eight characters) and then select **OK**. Like magic, the new directory is created.

Can I Destroy a Directory If I Want?

You can delete a directory you don't need any more. For example, you can delete a directory that you accidentally created in the wrong spot on the directory tree. Or you might want to remove the directory for an application you no longer use. You can delete a directory with the amazingly versatile File Manager.

Before you delete a directory, make sure you have the necessary copies of any files in the directory you are going to delete. (The files must be deleted before the directory can be deleted.) Then, from the File Manager directory tree, highlight the directory you want to delete. Choose File Delete.

Another dialog box will appear. After making sure the correct directory is shown, select **OK**. A Confirm Directory Delete dialog box will appear, enabling you to double-check the directory. Select **OK** if it's the right one.

If files are in the directory, a Confirm File Delete dialog box appears for each file. You must select **OK** to delete each file before the directory can be deleted.

Confirming Every File Is a Pain The Delete Confirmation dialog box provides you a Yes to **A**ll command button to confirm the deletion of all files at once. Make sure you really want to delete all those files before you use this feature.

Making and destroying directories was easy, right? In the next lesson, you will learn how to find files when you lose them.

Lesson 15

The Disappearing File Trick– Where Did It Go?

I Can't Find Anything in This Mess

Soon, you'll have loads and loads of files and oodles of directories on your computer. You'll discover that finding a particular file can be a little frustrating. But before you pull all your hair out, listen to this: there is a command you can use to find those files that have drifted into Windows' abyss. It is File Search.

Search is sort of like the unsung hero of the File menu. Oh sure, it's not as popular as Open or Exit, but I personally guarantee that there will be more than one time you'll be thankful for it.

You can search for either a single file or a group of files with similar names using the File Search command. To search for a group of files, use the *wild card* * (asterisk) with a partial file name to narrow down the search. You can use the wild card in place of characters you can't remember. Table 15.1 shows some search examples so you can get the hang of this wild card thingamajig.

Table 15.1 Searching with Wild cards

Characters Entered For Search	Sample Search Results
rpt1.wri (no wild card)	rpt1.wri
rpt*.wri	rpt1.wri, rpt2.wri, rpt11.wri (all rpt

continues

Table 15.1   Continued

Characters Entered For Search	Sample Search Results
	files with .wri extension)
c*.exe	calc.exe, calendar.exe (all files that start with a c and have an .exe extension)
*.exe	calc.exe, calendar.exe, notepad.exe (all files with .exe extension)
c*.*	calc.exe, calendar.exe, class.wri (all files that start with a c)

I'm Sold on the Search Command

To search for a file, first make sure you are in **File Manager**. (File Manager's icon is in Program Manager's Main group.) Then, select File Search, and a dialog box will appear (see Figure 15.1). In the Search For text area, enter the characters to search for. Use wild cards to identify unknown characters.

	Search	
Search For:	rp*.*	
Start From:	C:\WINDOWS	
	☒ Search All Subdirectories	

OK
Cancel
Help

Figure 15.1   *The completed Search dialog box.*

If you really have no idea where the file is and you need to search the entire drive, type **C:** in the Start From text box, and make sure the Search All Subdirectories check box is active (an **X** in the check box). If you have some inkling of where the file might be and you want to search only a certain directory and its subdirectories, type the file name in the Start From text box. If you've narrowed it down to a single directory (no subdirectories), type it in the Start From text box and make sure the Search All Subdirectories check box is not active (no X in the check box).

After all that is finished, select **OK** to begin the search. A new window called Search Results will appear, showing the files that were found (see Figure 15.2).

Figure 15.2   *The search results.*

Remarkably easy, isn't it? You can just look at the Search Results window to see if the file is there. When you're finished with the window, you can close it like any other window.

Now that you know how to use File Manager's powerful and all-knowing File Search command, you are now ready to do exquisite stuff to your files, like copying, moving, deleting and renaming them.

Lesson 16

File Finagling

The Art of Fine File Finagling

Before you can move, copy, rename, or delete files or directories, you must learn how to identify, or *select,* the ones you want. You can simply click on the item you want, or you can use the keys in Table 16.1 to select things.

Table 16.1 Keys to Select a File or Directory

Use This Key	To Select
≠	Previous file or directory
Ø	Next file or directory
→	Subdirectory or file to the right
←	Higher level directory or file to the left
Home	First file or directory
End	Last file or directory
First letter	Next file or directory of the name starting with a given letter
Tab	The next directory window

To really liven things up, you can select multiple files and then execute commands that will affect the entire group. For example, you can select several files to be copied to a disk, which is much faster than copying each file individually.

If all the files are in order (or *contiguous*) in the **File Manager** directory window, it's easy to select them. First, you have to click on the first file or directory that you want to select. (It becomes highlighted when you click on it.) Then, hold down the **Shift** key, and click on the last file or directory in the group that you want to select. All the items between the first and last selections are highlighted (including the first and last selections themselves).

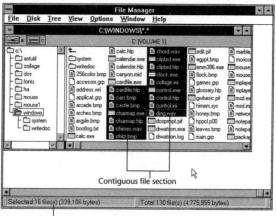

Contiguous file section

Status line

Figure 16.1   Selecting contiguous files.

If you're using the keyboard, use the arrow keys to move the highlight to the first file or directory that you want to select. Hold down the **Shift** key and use

the arrow keys to extend the highlight to the last file
or directory you want to select.

Tip

My Files Aren't in Order   Often, the files or directories you want to select are separated by unwanted
files. To select them, hold down the **Ctrl** key while you
click on them with the mouse. If you're using the
keyboard, press **Shift+F8**, and then use the arrow
keys to move to the items you want, and toggle them
on or off with the **Spacebar**. When you're done
selecting, press **Shift+F8** again.

How Do I Move and Copy Stuff?

To move or copy files or directories through the File
Manager, you *drag and drop*—that is, you select the
items you want from your *source* directory, drag them
to the *destination* directory, and then drop them there
by releasing the mouse button.

Before you move or copy, make sure the *source*
directory window is visible, so you can highlight the
file(s) that you're going to drag. Also, make sure that
the *destination* drive or directory is visible, either as an
open window or as an icon.

Tip

**It's Hot In Here, Let's Open More
Windows**   Here's a trick to use if you need more
windows. If you're copying between two directories,
you can open both directory windows using the
Window **N**ew Window command. It's usually easier
to tile the windows with **W**indow **T**ile so you can see
them both.

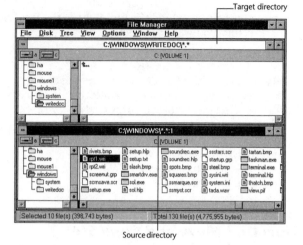

Figure 16.2   Two windows ready for moving or copying files.

To copy files or directories with the mouse, first select them. Then, holding down the **Ctrl** key, drag the items to the destination drive, directory, or icon. When you release the mouse button and the Ctrl key, a dialog box appears asking you to confirm the copy. Click on **OK**.

With the keyboard, choose File Copy after you've selected the rascals. The Copy dialog box appears, with selected files listed in the From text box. Type the desired destination in the To text box, including the path to the destination drive and directory. (Figure 16.3 shows a completed Copy dialog box.) Press **Enter**, and the files are copied.

Copy	
Current Directory: C:\WINDOWS	**OK**
From: RPT1.WRI RPT2.WRI	**Cancel**
To: ⦿ c:\windows\writedoc	
○ Copy to Clipboard	**Help**

Figure 16.3   The Copy dialog box completed.

To move things, all you have to do is select them, then drag them to the item you want to move them to and drop them. When the dialog box appears asking you to confirm the move, click on OK.

With the keyboard, choose File Move after you've selected the right things. In the dialog box, the selected files or directories are listed in the From text box. Type the desired destination in the To text box, including the path to the destination drive and directory. Then just press **Enter**.

How Do I Rename Files or Directories?

To rename your files, select the file or directory to rename, then choose File Rename. When the Rename dialog box appears, type in the new name for the file or directory in the To text box. Then select **OK**.

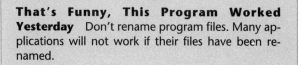

That's Funny, This Program Worked Yesterday Don't rename program files. Many applications will not work if their files have been renamed.

How Do I Delete Files or Directories?

You can delete files or directories, but be careful. Before you delete anything, it is a good idea to make a backup copy of any files or directories you might need later.

To delete, select the file or directory to delete , and then choose File Delete. In the Delete dialog box, check them carefully to make certain you are deleting what you intended to delete. When you select **OK**, you will be asked to confirm the deletion. Windows takes this deletion stuff very seriously. If you are deleting a directory and there are files which must be deleted first, you will be asked to confirm each file deletion.

If you've gotten through this whole lesson, you can consider yourself an experienced file finagler. Turn the page to continue to enhance your File Manager skills by learning how to format and copy floppy disks.

Lesson 17

Flipping Your Floppies—The Ever Enjoyable Task of Formatting and Copying Floppy Disks

You Can't Use It Unless It's Formatted

I know, I know, *formatting* disks sounds like about as much fun as stapling your toes together. But it's one of those little things in life that just has to be done. When you buy a box of floppy disks, the disks are usually unformatted. (You can buy formatted disks, but they're more expensive.) They're sold unformatted because some computers use operating systems other than DOS, and such systems need to format the floppy disks in their own format.

> **Recycle Your Disks** You can format and reformat a floppy disk as often as you want. If you format a previously used floppy disk, you'll erase all the stuff that was on it before, so make sure you don't need any of it any more.

Disks can be formatted from the DOS command line, but it's much more convenient to format disks from within the Windows' File Manager if you're already in Windows. After you insert the floppy disk into the drive, go to **File Manager** and choose Disk Format Disk. The Format Disk dialog box appears (see Figure 17.1).

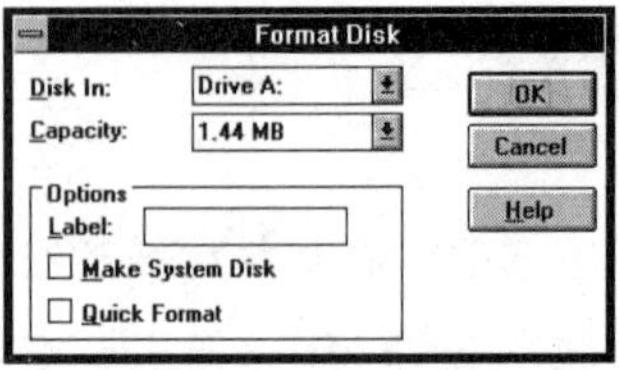

Figure 17.1 *The Format Disk dialog box.*

Use the Disk In drop-down list to select the drive the floppy disk is in. Then use the drop-down list to select the Capacity. (Look at Table 17.1 if you're confused about your capacity choices.) When you select OK, a confirmation box appears. Carefully check the information, and then select OK.

The disk drive lights up during formatting and a message appears on your screen identifying how much of the formatting process is complete. When the process is over, the Format Complete dialog box appears, telling you how much space is available on the newly formatted floppy disk and asking if you want to format another floppy disk. Select Yes to format another, or No to stop formatting.

Table 17.1 Floppy Disk Capacity to Specify when Formatting

Disk Diameter	Disk Density	Capacities Available
3.5-inch	Double	720KB
3.5-inch	High	1.44MB
5.25-inch	Double	360KB
5.25-inch	High	360KB or 1.2MB

> **Hey, My Disk Won't Format** If the floppy disk has errors that prevent it from being formatted, Windows will tell you. Pitch any floppy disks that cannot be formatted or have problems during the formatting process; they're unusable. You can format a high-density 5.25-inch floppy disk at either 360KB or 1.2MB capacity, but if you try to format a high-density 3.5-inch disk at 720KB capacity, Windows will (falsely) tell you the disk has errors. Windows hasn't lost its marbles, it just doesn't know how to format a high-density 3.5-inch disk at 720KB capacity; don't try it, it won't work.

What the Heck Is a System Disk and Why Do I Need One?

A *system disk* contains operating system files you need to start your computer in case your hard disk fails. If your computer won't boot and you've got a system disk handy, you can start your computer from the floppy disk drive.

You should always have at least one system disk on hand in case something goes wrong. A hard disk problem—or an error in your startup files—can lock you out of your system. With a system disk, you can boot from the floppy drive, bypassing the hard drive (*and* the error) until the problem can be found and corrected. Brilliant, eh?

How Do I Know Which Size Disk to Use for the System Disk? If you have two floppy disk drives (A and B) of differing sizes (5.25-inch and 3.5-inch), your system disk *must* be the kind that fits on drive A (usually the 5.25-inch one). The computer checks drive A first for a disk, and if it finds none, it boots from the hard disk. It never checks drive B when booting, so don't even think about trying to boot from there.

You can create a system disk when you format the floppy disk by checking the Make System Disk check box in the Format Disk dialog box.

If you've already formatted a disk that you want to make into a system disk, select the icon for your hard disk from File Manager's directory window. Insert a formatted floppy disk into drive A, and choose Disk Make System Disk. When the Make System Disk dialog box appears, select OK.

It's a good idea to create a system disk for your computer and store it in a safe place. Someday you might be glad you took this precaution.

Why Is File Manager Better for Copying Files Than DOS?

There are two kinds of people in this world: the kind that always do things the same way because that's what they're used to and they're downright stubborn, and the kind that constantly look for easier ways to do things. A member of the latter category, I long ago said good-bye to DOS' *diskcopy* command and started using File Manager to copy disks. Unlike DOS, File Manager does not require you to swap disks repeatedly when copying disks with higher capacities than 360KB. If you find swapping disks five or six times as annoying as I do, then you're ready to try File Manager's Disk Copy Disk command.

File Manager is great for copying *all* the files on one floppy disk to another. The only condition is that both floppy disks must be of the same capacity. For example, if the source floppy disk is 1.44MB (high density), the destination floppy disk must also be 1.44MB.

Which Is Which?   The *source* floppy disk is the one you are copying from. The *destination* floppy disk is the one you are copying to.

To copy a floppy disk, place the source floppy disk in the drive to copy *from*. If you have two drives of the same size and capacity, place the destination floppy disk in the drive to copy *to*. From the File Manager, select the drive of the source floppy disk, and then choose Disk Copy Disk.

A message appears reminding you that all the files on the destination floppy disk will be erased. Select Yes to go on. If you are using one drive, Windows will instruct you when to swap the source and destination floppy disks. Follow the instructions.

Well, you've conquered the formidable formatting and copying tasks, and somewhere in there, you also learned how to create a system disk.

Lesson 18

Copying, Cutting, and Pasting Between Windows

How Do I Move Stuff From One Document to Another?

One of the handiest features of Windows is that information (both text and graphics) can be copied or moved from one window to another. This includes documents in the same application as well as documents in a different application. When information is copied or cut, it is placed in an area called the *Clipboard*.

The Clipboard is kind of like one of those storage rooms you can rent when you run out of space in your garage. You move stuff to the Clipboard by using the Cut and Copy commands on the Edit menu. Then when you are ready to move it out of the Clipboard into a new position, you use the Edit menu's Paste command.

Can I Put All Sorts of Things in the Clipboard?
The Clipboard runs out of room fast. It can only hold the most recent information that you copied or cut. When you copy or cut something else, it replaces what was previously on the Clipboard. And when you turn off your computer or exit Windows, everything in the Clipboard is lost!

What's the Difference Between Cutting and Copying?   When you *cut* information, it is deleted from its original location and placed on the Clipboard. When you *copy* information, it is copied to the Clipboard without disturbing the original.

I Can't Remember What's in the Clipboard

If you want to see what you've put in the Clipboard, you can look at it through a program in Program Manager's Main group. First, go to the Program Manager window, then open the Main group icon. From the Main window, open the Clipboard Viewer program-item icon. The contents of the Clipboard will appear in the Clipboard Viewer window.

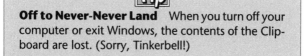

Off to Never-Never Land   When you turn off your computer or exit Windows, the contents of the Clipboard are lost. (Sorry, Tinkerbell!)

But How Do I Use the Clipboard if I Don't Know How To Cut or Copy?

Cutting and copying text is simple and painless as long as you know how to *select* text. When you select text, you highlight it so that Windows can identify the text you are trying to manipulate (cut, copy, or paste). Figure 18.1 illustrates selected text in a Write document.

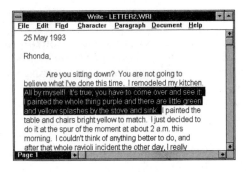

Figure 18.1 *Selected text in a Write document.*

Your mouse pointer will look like a capital *I* when it is in an area where you can type text. When it looks like that, it is called, appropriately enough, an *I-beam*. To select text with the mouse, you first position the I-beam pointer just before the first character to be selected. Then, you hold down the left mouse button and drag the I-beam pointer to the last character to be selected. When you release the mouse button, the selected text is highlighted.

To select text with the keyboard, use the arrow keys to position the insertion point (blinking vertical line) just before the first character to be selected. Hold down the Shift key and use the arrow keys to move the highlight to the last character to be selected. When you release all keys, the selected text is highlighted. Sometimes, this is faster, especially if you aren't completely mouse-literate or are using the keyboard a lot.

Oops, I Selected the Wrong Thing   To get rid of the highlighting, click anywhere else in the document. To get rid of the highlighting with the keyboard, press an arrow key.

There are some really cool tricks you can use to select text. For example, to select a single word using the mouse, double-click on the word. To select text word-by-word (instead of character-by-character), hold down both the **Shift** and **Ctrl** keys while using the arrow keys.

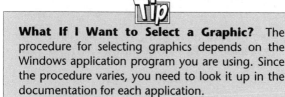

What If I Want to Select a Graphic? The procedure for selecting graphics depends on the Windows application program you are using. Since the procedure varies, you need to look it up in the documentation for each application.

My Text Is Selected, Now What?

Once you have selected the text or graphics, the way you cut, copy, and paste is the same in all Windows applications. If you're cutting or copying information between different windows (of the same application as well as between windows of different applications), you first open the Edit menu.

Then, choose Copy to keep the original selection in place or Cut to remove the original selection. The selected material is placed in the Clipboard. Position the I-beam or insertion point where you want to insert the selection. (You may need to open another application or document.)

Open the Edit menu, and choose Paste. The selection is copied from the Clipboard to your document. (A copy will remain on the Clipboard until you cut or copy something else.)

You can paste information from the clipboard many times over.

Tip

Could I Paste This Thing Twenty Times if I Want? Sure. Items remain on the Clipboard until you cut or copy again, you can paste information from the Clipboard multiple times. You can also perform other tasks in between pasting.

Now that you are a Cut, Copy, and Paste wizard, you're ready to learn how to use the Write Accessory.

Lesson 19

Write: The Shakespeare of Windows Accessories

So, I Can Write Stuff with This Thing?

You can use Write to create letters, memos, reports, novels, ransom notes, and so on. Write is a pretty easy word processor to use.

To use the program, first you have to find the Write program-item icon. It's in Program Manager's Accessories group. Open the program, and you'll see the Write window (shown in Figure 19.1). It will look like a big empty sheet of paper.

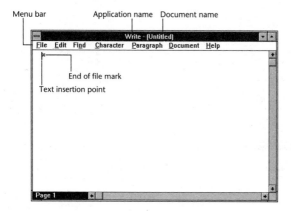

Figure 19.1 *The Windows Write window.*

Is Entering Text as Easy As Just Typing What I Want?

Usually, entering text is incredibly easy. All you have to do is begin typing. Just remember this: do not press Enter at the end of each line or else you'll go around making thousands of separate paragraphs and generally wreaking havoc on your document. Just allow the text to automatically wrap around and press **Enter** only when you want to mark the end of a paragraph.

Your mouse pointer will be an I-beam when it is positioned in a place where you can type. If you want to move the cursor to a new place, just move the I-beam and click.

Figure 19.2 shows my Write screen after I've written a letter to my friend.

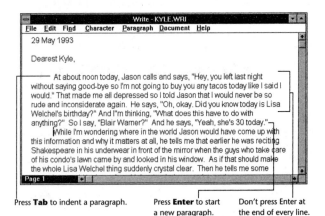

Press **Tab** to indent a paragraph.   Press **Enter** to start   Don't press Enter at
a new paragraph.   the end of every line.

Figure 19.2   Text typed in the Write document.

What If I Change My Mind about What I've Typed?

Editing your documents is easy. You can move around with the keys listed in Table 19.1, or you can just click on the place you want with the mouse.

Table 19.1 Moving Around with the Keyboard

Key	Movement
↓	Down a line
↑	Up a line
→	Right one character
←	Left one character
PageUp	Previous screen
PageDown	Next screen
Ctrl+←	Previous word
Ctrl+→	Next word
Ctrl+PageUp	Top of screen
Ctrl+PageDown	Bottom of screen
Home	Start of line
End	End of line
Ctrl+Home	Start of document
Ctrl+End	End of document

If you're just dying to add text to what you've already typed, move the insertion point and begin typing. The existing characters will move to the right as you type in new text.

Change a Whole Bunch at Once

You can edit a block of text, but you first need to select it (highlight it). If you're using the mouse, put the mouse pointer at the start of the text you want to select, then press and hold down the mouse button and drag the mouse over the stuff you want. When everything you want is highlighted, release the mouse button. Now you can perform commands on the highlighted material.

Can I Select an Entire Paragraph? When you move the mouse pointer slightly to the left side of the Write window, it changes into an arrow that points sort of northeast. If it looks like that, you can click the mouse button to select the entire line it's on, or double-click to select the entire paragraph.

If you're using the keyboard, place the insertion point to the left of the first character, then press and hold down the **Shift** key. Move the insertion point to the last character in the selection, and release the Shift key.

Can I Select the Entire Document? Press **Ctrl+Home** to move the insertion point to the beginning of the document. Hold down the **Shift** and **Ctrl** keys and press the **End** key (**Shift+Ctrl+End**).

Going, Going, Gone

To delete a single character, press the **Backspace** key to delete the character to the left. Press the **Delete** key to delete the character to the right. To delete larger amounts of text, select the text then press the **Delete** key.

Switcheroo

Copying and moving stuff is easy once you've selected it. Just choose Edit Copy, or Cut from the menu bar. Place your insertion point where you want to paste the text, then choose Edit Paste.

I Need Some Variety

You can affect the appearance of your document by changing the *formatting*. Formatting refers to the appearance of a document, including character style and font, line spacing, and page layout.

Use the Character menu to select the style you want for your text. Write has five basic character styles (Bold, Italic, Underline, Superscript, and Subscript). If you select one of these things and then type your text, the text will appear on-screen in the style you want. To format existing text, just highlight the text and then choose from the Character menu.

I Already Typed the Text I Want to Format If you want to change the character style of existing text, highlight the text, and then set the character style using the **C**haracter menu.

You can also change the fonts that are used in your document. Select Character Fonts to access the Fonts dialog box, shown in Figure 19.3. You can choose a font before you enter the text, or you can select text you've entered and change the font.

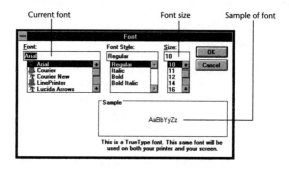

Figure 19.3   The Font dialog box.

I Need More Room

You can adjust the margins and the line spacing of your document if you want more or less information to fit on one page.

The default margins are 1" for the top and bottom margins and 1.25" for the right and left margins, but you don't have to use those if you don't want to. You can change margins using the Document Page Layout command. Just type the margins you want to use, and select **OK**.

To change line spacing, put the insertion point in the paragraph to change. From the Paragraph menu, choose **Single Space**, **1 1/2 Space**, or **Double Space**.

Save It for Later

Whether you are creating a Write document or another type of document file, *always* save your work often. In Write, choose File Save. If the document *has not* been saved before, the Save As dialog box. Select the directory you want to save the document in, and enter the name you want to assign to the document, and then select **OK**.

If the document *has* been saved before, Write will simply save the changes you made. You will be returned to the document window to continue your work or to exit once the document is saved.

Let's Print This Baby

You've been slaving away for hours on your Write document and finally you're ready to print. Choose File Print, and the Print dialog box appears. Identify the number of copies (if more than one) and the pages to print (if applicable), and select **OK**. A dialog box appears to let you know the document is printing. To cancel the print job, press **Cancel**.

When What You See Is Not What You Get If there are formatting or document appearance problems, your problem is within the Write document. Double check your work.

In this lesson, you learned how to use the Write Accessory. Give yourself a reward and learn to use Paintbrush! You'll be embarrassed by how much fun adults can have with the Paintbrush Accessory.

Lesson 20

Paintbrush: The Picasso of Windows Accessories

Using Paintbrush Is Better Than Finger Painting in Kindergarten

To open Paintbrush, select its program-item icon from the **Accessories** group window in **Program Manager**. The Paintbrush screen shown in Figure 20.1 will appear. Think of the screen as a bare canvas that you can paint on.

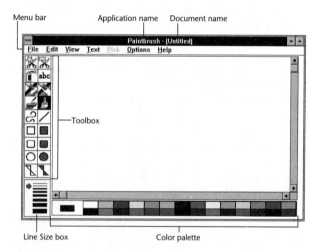

Figure 20.1 *The Paintbrush screen.*

In addition to familiar window parts, the Paintbrush window shown in Figure 20.1 has a set of drawing tools (called the *toolbox*) on the left along with a *color palette* on the bottom of the window.

What Does This Box in the Color Pallette Do?
The box within a box to the left of the color palette shows the currently selected *foreground* and *background* colors. The foreground color (the smaller box) is the color you'll use when you draw, and the background color is the color of the backdrop.

The *line size box* on the lower left of the window identifies the width of a line when you draw. Figure 20.2 shows each of the tools in the toolbox.

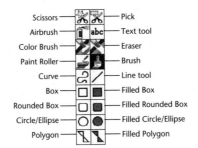

Figure 20.2   The tools in the toolbox.

All the Joy of Painting with None of the Mess

Painting is such fun when you use the mouse. (You can use the keyboard, but all the cool people use the mouse because it's much easier. I'm not going to explain how to use the keyboard here because you wouldn't like it anyway.) Follow these guidelines whilst creating:

☞ To select the background color, point at a color in the palette, and click the right mouse button.

☞ To select the foreground color, point at the color in the palette, and click the left mouse button.

☞ To select the size of your drawing, choose Options Image Attributes, and enter the Width and Height in the Image Attributes dialog box.

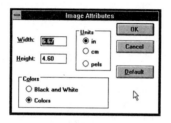

Figure 20.3   The Image Attributes dialog box.

To open a new document with the settings you just entered while following the preceding guidelines, choose File New. To start drawing, first select a drawing tool from the toolbox at the left of the screen. Select the line width by clicking on the line size in the box in the lower left of the screen. To draw an object, point at the area where you want the object to appear, and drag the mouse pointer until the object is the size you want.

Rats! If you add to your graphic and decide you don't like the addition, choose **E**dit **U**ndo (or press **Alt+Backspace**) to undo the change you made. Use this option carefully, since all changes you have made since you last changed tools will be undone.

A Perfect Circle Every Time To draw a perfect circle with the Ellipse tool, hold down the **Shift** key as you drag the mouse pointer. This technique can also be used to help you draw a perfect square and a perfectly straight line with the tools associated with them.

A Touch of Text

To add text to a graphic, select the **Text** tool, then choose Text Font. From the Font dialog box, select the Font, Font Style, and Size, and select OK. You can't edit text once it's placed in your drawing, so make sure everything is correct before selecting OK. Place the insertion point where you want it, then type the text.

Once You Leave, You Can Never Get Back You can't edit text once you have accepted it; you can only erase it with the Eraser tool. Because of this, be sure that what you've typed is correct before you move on.

Figure 20.4 displays a graphic with text created in Paintbrush. The selected Font is Arial (supplied by Windows). The Font Style is Bold. The Size is 18.

Figure 20.4   *My self-portrait masterpiece with added text.*

Save and Print the Masterpiece

To save the drawing, choose File Save. If the file has not been saved before, choose a directory to save it in, name it, and select OK.

To print the drawing, choose File Print. Complete the Print dialog box, and then select **OK**.

So, did you have loads of fun and while away the hours with Paintbrush? In the next lesson, you'll learn how to keep track of those hours with the Calendar Accessory.

Lesson 21

Counting the Days with the Calendar and the Clock

Why Should I Use the Calendar?

Windows' Calendar is handy to keep track of your daily or monthly schedule. Maintaining appointments, birthdays, holidays, and deadlines with the Calendar can help organize your life. And, if you tend to get engrossed with your work at the computer and forget the time, you can set an alarm to tell you when to quit.

To use the Calendar, open the **Calendar** icon from Program Manager's **Accessories** group. A screen like the one shown in Figure 21.1 appears.

Choose View, Month, or Day to view the current month or current day display. Figure 21.1 displays the Day View. To view a day from a month calendar view, select the day and press **Enter**.

From a day calendar, you may view or edit the information for the day. You may also set an alarm for the time line where your insertion point rests. Choose Alarm Set to set an alarm for a particular time. Select Show, and then select Today, Previous, Next, or Date to change days.

When you are done using the Calendar, choose File Save, enter a file name, and choose OK. To leave the Calendar, choose File, Exit.

Table 21.1 lists shortcut keys you can use to move around in the Calendar.

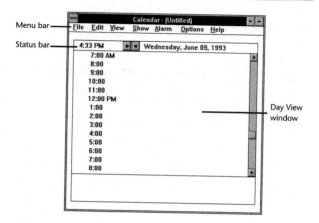

Figure 21.1 *The Calendar screen: the Day View.*

Table 21.1 Calendar's Shortcut Keys

Shortcut Key Sequence	Description
F8	Displays day view
F9	Displays month view
Ctrl+PageDown	Display next month/day
Ctrl+PageUp	Displays previous month/day
F5	Set alarm on day and time

Double-click in the status bar of the calendar (with the date) to switch between Day and Month View.

It Would Be Nice If I Could Print This Out

You can print out your appointments on the Calendar. Choose File Print. The Print dialog box, shown in Figure 21.2, appears. Enter the date to print From and To, then select OK.

Figure 21.2   The Calendar's Print dialog box.

What's With This Clock Thingy?

Windows' Clock can keep you on time. It may be displayed as an analog clock (see Figure 21.3) or a digital clock (see Figure 21.4).

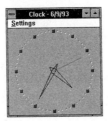

Figure 21.3   The analog clock.

To use the Clock, open the **Clock** icon from Program Manager's **Accessories** group. To switch between analog and digital display, choose **Settings** Analog, or Digital. Close the clock using the **Control** menu.

Figure 21.4   The digital clock.

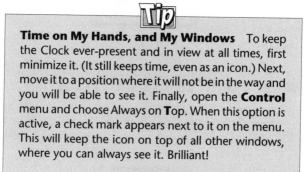

Time on My Hands, and My Windows   To keep the Clock ever-present and in view at all times, first minimize it. (It still keeps time, even as an icon.) Next, move it to a position where it will not be in the way and you will be able to see it. Finally, open the **Control** menu and choose Always on **T**op. When this option is active, a check mark appears next to it on the menu. This will keep the icon on top of all other windows, where you can always see it. Brilliant!

In this lesson, you learned how to manage your precious time with the Calendar. Guess what? There are no more lessons. You've covered the very least you need to know about Windows. Now put this book in your pocket, sit back and bask in your newfound knowledge.

Index

Other Idiot-Proof Books from Alpha!

If you enjoyed this Complete Idiot's Pocket Guide, then you may want to check out the rest!

Complete Idiot's Pocket Guides

The Complete Idiot's
Pocket Guide to DOS 6
ISBN: 1-56761-303-9
Softbound, $5.99 USA

The Complete Idiot's
Pocket Guide to Windows
(version 3.1)
ISBN: 1-56761-302-0
Softbound, $5.99 USA

The Complete Idiot's
Pocket Guide to
WordPerfect 6
ISBN: 1-56761-300-4
Softbound, $5.99 USA

The Complete Idiot's
Pocket Guide to Word for
Windows (version 2)
ISBN: 1-56761-301-2
Softbound, $5.99 USA

If you can't find these books at your local computer book retailer, call this toll-free number for more information! 1-800-428-5331